Acadia National Park Travel Guide 2024-2025

Your Comprehensive Handbook to Experiencing the Beauty and Charm of Maine's Coastal Gem

Kelly J. Cloutier

Copyright © 2024 by Kelly J. Cloutier

All rights reserved. No part of this book may be reproduced, stored in a retrieval system, or transmitted in any form or by any means—electronic, mechanical, photocopying, recording, or otherwise—without prior written permission of the author, except in the case of brief quotations embodied in critical articles and reviews.

Disclaimer

The information contained in this travel guide is for general information purposes only. While the author endeavors to keep the information up to date and correct, there are no representations or warranties, express or implied, about the completeness, accuracy, reliability, suitability, or availability with respect to the guide or the information, products, services, or related graphics contained in the guide for any purpose. Any reliance you place on such information is therefore strictly at your own risk.

In no event will the author be liable for any loss or damage including without limitation, indirect or consequential loss or damage, or any loss or damage whatsoever arising from loss of data or profits arising out of, or in connection with, the use of this guide.

Through this guide, you may be able to link to other websites which are not under the control of the author. The author has no control over the nature, content, and availability of those sites. The inclusion of any links does not necessarily imply a recommendation or endorse the views expressed within them.

Contents

Introduction to Acadia National Park...................... 6
Overview of the Park.. 6
History and Significance.. 8
Unique Features and Highlights... 10

Chapter 1: Planning Your Trip............................... 14
How to Get There.. 14
Accommodation Options... 16
Transportation Within the Park... 19
Sample Itineraries... 21

Chapter 2: When to Visit... 26
Seasonal Highlights.. 26
Weather Considerations.. 28
Special Events and Festivals... 31
Best Times for Specific Activities.. 34

Chapter 3: Budgeting for Your Trip....................... 39
Cost Breakdown.. 39
Money-Saving Tips... 41
Affordable Accommodation and Dining Options................ 43
Free and Low-Cost Activities.. 44

Chapter 4: Essentials for Traveling........................ 48
Packing List.. 48
Health and Safety Tips... 51
Travel Insurance... 54

Communication and Connectivity.. 56
Chapter 5: Entry and Visa Requirements................ 60
Visa Information for International Visitors............................ 60
Park Entry Fees and Passes.. 63
Registration and Permits for Specific Activities.................... 66
Chapter 6: Exploring the Park.. 72
Top Hiking Trails.. 72
Scenic Drives... 76
Wildlife Watching.. 79
Water Activities.. 82
Chapter 7: Cultural Experiences.............................. 86
Local History and Traditions.. 86
Museums and Cultural Centers... 88
Local Cuisine and Dining Experiences................................... 91
Art and Craft Markets... 93
Chapter 8: Family-Friendly Activities...................... 96
Kid-Friendly Hikes and Trails.. 96
Educational Programs and Junior Ranger Activities........... 99
Best Picnic Spots and Play Areas.. 101
Chapter 9: Accommodations & Luxury Hotels...... 106
Budget-Friendly Hotels... 108
Restaurants... 110
Chapter 10: 5-Day Itinerary...................................... 112
Day 1: Arrival and Exploration.. 112
Day 2: Hiking and Sightseeing... 113
Day 3: Wildlife and Water Activities..................................... 114

Day 4: Cultural and Historical Sites.. 115
Day 5: Relaxation and Departure... 116
Chapter 11: Sustainable Travel Tips........................ 118
Leave No Trace Principles... 118
Eco-Friendly Accommodation and Dining........................... 121
Supporting Local Communities... 123
Reducing Your Carbon Footprint.. 125

Introduction to Acadia National Park

Overview of the Park

Acadia National Park, located along the rugged coast of Maine, is one of the most visited and cherished national parks in the United States. Encompassing over 49,000 acres, it includes a diverse landscape of rocky shorelines, dense forests, and granite peaks, most notably Cadillac Mountain, which is the highest point on the U.S. East Coast. The park is known for its stunning vistas, abundant wildlife, and a myriad of recreational opportunities that attract millions of visitors each year.

Established as a national park in 1919, Acadia has grown through land donations and acquisitions to protect its unique and fragile ecosystems. Its proximity to the Atlantic Ocean creates a unique climate that supports a rich variety of plant and animal life, making it a paradise for nature enthusiasts. From the vibrant colors of autumn foliage to the serene beauty of a sunrise over the ocean, Acadia offers an ever-changing landscape that captivates visitors.

The park is easily accessible from the nearby town of Bar Harbor, which serves as a gateway with ample amenities, including lodging, dining, and shopping. This charming town provides a perfect base for exploring the park's many trails, scenic drives, and historic sites. Whether you are a hiker, biker, kayaker, or simply a lover of natural beauty,

Acadia National Park promises an unforgettable experience.

History and Significance

The history of Acadia National Park is a tale of conservation, philanthropy, and a deep appreciation for natural beauty. The area now known as Acadia was originally inhabited by the Wabanaki people, whose presence dates back over 12,000 years. They thrived on the abundant resources provided by the land and sea, leaving behind a rich cultural legacy that is still evident today.

In the late 19th and early 20th centuries, the beauty of the Mount Desert Island region began to attract wealthy summer visitors, including prominent figures like John D. Rockefeller Jr., George B. Dorr, and Charles W. Eliot. These individuals played pivotal roles in the conservation movement that led to the creation of the park. Rockefeller, in particular, contributed significantly by financing and overseeing the construction of the park's famous carriage roads, a network of gravel roads designed for horse-drawn carriages that are still used by hikers and bikers today.

The park's establishment was driven by the vision and efforts of George B. Dorr, often called the "Father of Acadia National Park." Dorr dedicated his life to acquiring and protecting the land, ultimately leading to the designation of the area as a national monument in 1916 and its subsequent establishment as Lafayette National Park in 1919. It was renamed Acadia National Park in 1929 to honor the French heritage of the region.

The significance of Acadia extends beyond its natural beauty. It represents one of the earliest successful conservation efforts in the United States, setting a precedent for future national parks. The park's establishment marked a commitment to preserving natural landscapes for public enjoyment and education, a legacy that continues to inspire conservation efforts worldwide.

Unique Features and Highlights

Acadia National Park is renowned for its distinctive and diverse features that offer visitors a wealth of natural wonders to explore. One of the park's most iconic landmarks is Cadillac Mountain. At 1,530 feet, it is the tallest peak on the U.S. Atlantic coast and offers breathtaking views, especially at sunrise. During certain times of the year, it is the first place in the United States to see the sunrise, making it a popular destination for early risers.

The park's 27-mile Park Loop Road provides a scenic drive that highlights many of Acadia's most spectacular sights, including Sand Beach, Thunder Hole, and Otter Cliff. Sand Beach is a unique coastal feature nestled between rocky headlands, offering a rare sandy shoreline perfect for sunbathing and swimming. Thunder Hole, named for the thunderous sound created when waves crash into a naturally formed inlet, is a must-see for its dramatic displays of ocean power.

Jordan Pond, another highlight, is known for its clear waters and the picturesque view of the Bubble Mountains. The Jordan Pond House, located nearby, is famous for its popovers and tea, providing a quintessential Acadian experience. The pond's surrounding trails offer opportunities for leisurely walks and more challenging hikes, catering to all levels of outdoor enthusiasts.

Acadia's extensive network of carriage roads, totaling 45 miles, is a testament to Rockefeller's vision and remains a beloved feature of the park. These roads, free of motorized vehicles, are perfect for walking, biking, and horseback riding, offering tranquil paths through the park's forests and around its lakes and mountains.

Wildlife watching is another highlight, with the park's diverse habitats supporting species such as moose, black bears, white-tailed deer, and numerous bird species. The rocky coastline is also home to seals, porpoises, and various marine birds, making it a prime location for observing marine life.

Acadia's dark skies offer stargazers a chance to see the Milky Way and other celestial wonders, with the annual Acadia Night Sky Festival celebrating the region's commitment to preserving its pristine night skies.

Acadia National Park's unique combination of natural beauty, rich history, and diverse recreational opportunities makes it a premier destination for visitors seeking both adventure and tranquility. Its iconic landmarks, scenic drives, and commitment to conservation ensure that it remains a cherished treasure for generations to come.

Chapter 1: Planning Your Trip

How to Get There

Acadia National Park, located primarily on Mount Desert Island in Maine, is accessible through various modes of transportation, making it a convenient destination for travelers from across the United States and beyond.

By Air: The closest major airport to Acadia National Park is Bangor International Airport (BGR), situated about 50 miles from the park.

Bangor International Airport offers flights from major cities in the U.S., making it a suitable gateway for those flying in. From the airport, you can rent a car or use shuttle services to reach the park. Another option is the Hancock County-Bar Harbor Airport (BHB), located approximately 10 miles from the park's entrance. Although smaller, it provides seasonal flights and is much closer to the park.

By Car: Driving to Acadia offers the flexibility to explore the surrounding areas at your own pace. From Boston, the drive is around 5 hours via I-95 North, while from New York City, it takes about 8-9 hours. The scenic routes along the coast of Maine, especially U.S. Route 1, provide picturesque views and quaint towns worth exploring en route to the park.

By Bus: For those who prefer not to drive, several bus services operate routes to Bar Harbor, the main town adjacent to Acadia. Concord Coach Lines offers direct services from Boston to Bangor, with connections to Bar Harbor. Downeast Transportation also provides seasonal bus services from Bangor to Bar Harbor, making it a viable option for travelers relying on public transport.

By Train: While there are no direct train services to Acadia, Amtrak's Downeaster service connects Boston to Brunswick, Maine. From Brunswick, you can rent a car or take a bus to complete the journey to Acadia National Park.

By Ferry: If you're coming from Canada, the CAT ferry operates between Nova Scotia and Bar Harbor, providing a unique and scenic approach to the park. This ferry service is seasonal and offers a convenient connection for Canadian visitors.

Accommodation Options

Acadia National Park and the surrounding areas offer a wide range of accommodation options to suit various preferences and budgets.

Camping: For an immersive experience, camping within the park is a popular choice. Acadia has several campgrounds, including Blackwoods, Seawall, and Schoodic Woods. Blackwoods Campground is open year-round and is located close to many of the park's main attractions. Seawall Campground, situated on the quieter western side of the island, offers a more rustic experience. Schoodic Woods Campground, located on the Schoodic Peninsula, provides a serene environment away from the more crowded areas of the park. Reservations are highly recommended, especially during peak seasons.

Lodges and Inns: Bar Harbor, the nearest town, offers numerous lodges and inns ranging from budget-friendly to luxurious. The iconic Bar Harbor Inn & Spa provides stunning waterfront views and top-notch amenities. Other notable options include the Bluenose Inn, known for its panoramic views of Frenchman Bay, and the Atlantic Oceanside Hotel & Conference Center, which offers family-friendly accommodations.

Bed and Breakfasts: For a more intimate and charming stay, consider one of the many bed and breakfasts in Bar Harbor and the surrounding towns. These establishments often provide personalized service and a cozy atmosphere. Some popular options include the Yellow House Bed and Breakfast and the Anne's White Columns Inn.

Vacation Rentals: If you prefer a home-like environment, vacation rentals are widely available through platforms like Airbnb and VRBO. Options range from quaint cottages to luxurious homes, offering the flexibility to cook your meals and enjoy more privacy.

Budget Hotels and Motels: For budget-conscious travelers, there are several motels and budget hotels in Bar Harbor and nearby towns. These establishments provide basic amenities and are often conveniently located near the park entrances.

Hostels: Hostel accommodations, though limited, are available for those looking for a more affordable and social experience. The Bar Harbor Hostel, for example, offers dormitory-style accommodations and is an excellent option for solo travelers or those on a tight budget.

Transportation Within the Park

Navigating Acadia National Park is straightforward, with various transportation options to suit different needs.

Private Vehicle: Driving your own car or a rental car provides the most flexibility to explore the park at your own pace. The Park Loop Road, a 27-mile scenic drive, is the primary route through the park, offering access to major attractions like Sand Beach, Thunder Hole, and Cadillac Mountain. Keep in mind that parking can be limited during peak seasons, so arriving early is advisable.

Island Explorer Shuttle Bus: During the summer and early fall, the Island Explorer Shuttle Bus offers a convenient and eco-friendly way to get around the park. This free shuttle service connects various points within the park, including campgrounds, trailheads, and popular sites, as well as Bar Harbor and other nearby communities. The shuttles are equipped with bike racks, making it easy to combine biking and hiking.

Biking: Acadia is a bike-friendly park, with 45 miles of carriage roads built by John D. Rockefeller Jr. These gravel roads are closed to motor vehicles and provide scenic, traffic-free routes through the park. Biking is an excellent way to explore the park's interior, and bikes can be rented in Bar Harbor if you don't bring your own.

Walking and Hiking: Many of Acadia's attractions are accessible via well-maintained hiking trails. The park has over 120 miles of hiking trails, ranging from easy walks to challenging climbs. Popular trails include the Jordan Pond Path, the Precipice Trail, and the Cadillac Mountain South Ridge Trail. Walking is often the best way to experience the park's natural beauty up close.

Horseback Riding: The carriage roads are also open to horseback riding. Several stables in the area offer guided rides, allowing visitors to experience the park from a different perspective.

Sample Itineraries

To help you make the most of your visit, here are sample itineraries for different trip lengths:

1-Day Itinerary:

- Morning: Start your day with a sunrise hike up Cadillac Mountain or drive to the summit for panoramic views.
- Mid-Morning: Visit Sand Beach and hike the Great Head Trail for stunning coastal views.
- Lunch: Enjoy a picnic at Jordan Pond House and indulge in their famous popovers.
- Afternoon: Explore the Jordan Pond Path and take in the serene beauty of the Bubble Mountains.
- Late Afternoon: Drive the Park Loop Road, stopping at Thunder Hole and Otter Cliff.
- Evening: Return to Bar Harbor for dinner and a stroll along the waterfront.

3-Day Itinerary:

Day 1: Follow the 1-Day Itinerary.

Day 2 Morning: Take a boat tour of Frenchman Bay for wildlife viewing and scenic landscapes.
- Mid-Morning: Explore the Carriage Roads by bike, starting at the Eagle Lake Carriage Road.
- Lunch: Have lunch in Bar Harbor at one of the local seafood restaurants.
- Afternoon: Hike the Beehive Trail for a challenging adventure with rewarding views.
- Evening: Attend a ranger-led evening program or stargaze at Cadillac Mountain.

Day 3 Morning: Drive to the Schoodic Peninsula and explore the less crowded area of the park.
- Mid-Morning: Hike the Schoodic Head Trail for panoramic views of the coastline.
- Lunch: Picnic at Schoodic Point with spectacular ocean views.
- Afternoon: Visit the nearby town of Winter Harbor and enjoy its quaint shops and galleries.

- Evening: Return to Bar Harbor for a relaxing dinner and explore the town's nightlife.

5-Day Itinerary:

Days 1-3: Follow the 3-Day Itinerary.

Day 4 Morning: Take a kayaking tour of the coastal waters around Mount Desert Island.

- Mid-Morning: Visit the Wild Gardens of Acadia and learn about the region's native plant species.
- Lunch: Enjoy lunch at a local café in Northeast Harbor.
- Afternoon: Hike the Asticou and Thuya Gardens, showcasing beautiful horticultural displays.
- Evening: Attend a concert or cultural event in Bar Harbor.

Day 5 Morning: Explore the Bass Harbor Head Lighthouse and hike the Ship Harbor Trail.

- Mid-Morning: Visit the Abbe Museum to learn about the Wabanaki people and their history.
- Lunch: Have lunch at a lobster pound for a quintessential Maine experience.
- Afternoon: Relax at Echo Lake Beach, a freshwater alternative to the park's coastal beaches.
- Evening: Enjoy a farewell dinner in Bar Harbor, reflecting on your adventures in Acadia.

These itineraries provide a balanced mix of sightseeing, outdoor activities, and cultural experiences, ensuring a memorable visit to Acadia National Park.

Chapter 2: When to Visit

Seasonal Highlights

Acadia National Park offers unique experiences throughout the year, each season bringing its own set of attractions and activities that highlight the park's natural beauty.

Spring (March to May): Spring is a season of renewal in Acadia. As the snow melts and the temperatures begin to rise, the park's flora comes back to life. Wildflowers such as lupines and lady's slippers bloom, adding splashes of color to the landscape. Migratory birds return, making it a prime time for birdwatching. Trails start to become accessible again, though some may still be muddy from melting snow. One of the less crowded times to visit, spring offers a peaceful atmosphere and the chance to see the park awakening from winter.

Summer (June to August): Summer is the peak season for Acadia National Park, drawing the largest number of visitors. The weather is warm and pleasant, with temperatures typically ranging from the mid-60s to mid-70s Fahrenheit. All park facilities are open, and a full range of activities are available. The Park Loop Road is fully accessible, and popular spots like Sand Beach, Thunder Hole, and Jordan Pond are bustling with activity. The park's lush greenery and long daylight hours make it ideal for hiking, biking, and water sports. Summer also brings a vibrant cultural scene in nearby Bar Harbor, with various events and festivals.

Fall (September to November): Fall is perhaps the most visually stunning season in Acadia. The foliage transforms into a tapestry of reds, oranges, and yellows, attracting leaf-peepers and photographers. The weather is cool and crisp, perfect for hiking and other outdoor activities. Autumn also tends to see fewer crowds than summer, offering a more tranquil experience. Peak foliage typically occurs in early to mid-October, though this can vary depending on the year. Fall is also harvest season, and local markets and restaurants feature an abundance of fresh, seasonal produce.

Winter (December to February): Winter in Acadia is a time of serene beauty. The park is transformed by snow and ice, offering a stark and peaceful landscape. While many facilities and roads, including the Park Loop Road, close for the season, this is the perfect time for winter sports enthusiasts. Activities such as cross-country skiing, snowshoeing, and winter hiking become popular. The Carriage Roads, free from motor vehicles, provide groomed trails for skiing. Winter also offers excellent conditions for stargazing, with clear, cold nights and minimal light pollution.

Weather Considerations

Understanding Acadia National Park's weather patterns is crucial for planning a successful visit. The park's coastal location means that weather can vary significantly from season to season and even day to day.

Spring: Early spring can still be quite chilly, with temperatures ranging from the 30s to 50s Fahrenheit. By May, temperatures generally rise to the 50s and 60s. Rain is common during spring, so packing waterproof gear is advisable. Trails can be muddy due to melting snow, so sturdy, waterproof footwear is essential. The variability in weather means visitors should be prepared for both warm, sunny days and cooler, wet conditions.

Summer: Summer offers the most stable and warmest weather, with daytime temperatures in the 60s to mid-70s Fahrenheit. Nights can be cooler, often dropping into the 50s, so bringing layers is recommended. The coastal location can also mean occasional fog and cooler breezes, especially in the morning and evening. Summer thunderstorms are possible, so it's wise to stay informed about weather forecasts and be prepared for sudden changes.

Fall: Fall temperatures start in the 60s and gradually drop to the 40s by November. This season can see varying weather, with crisp, clear days ideal for outdoor activities and cooler, damp days as winter approaches. Layers are key, as temperatures can fluctuate throughout the day. Fall also brings shorter daylight hours, so plan hikes and activities accordingly. The fall foliage season can attract significant numbers of visitors, so it's beneficial to plan ahead for accommodations and popular activities.

Winter: Winter in Acadia can be harsh, with temperatures ranging from the teens to 30s Fahrenheit. Snow and ice are common, so appropriate winter gear, including insulated clothing, snow boots, and traction devices for footwear, is essential. Many trails can be icy or snow-covered, making them challenging without the right equipment. Despite the cold, clear winter days can offer stunning views and excellent conditions for winter sports. Winter visitors should be prepared for the possibility of road closures and limited services within the park.

Special Events and Festivals

Acadia National Park and the surrounding communities host a variety of events and festivals throughout the year that can enhance your visit.

Acadia Night Sky Festival (September): This annual festival celebrates the stunning night skies of Acadia, which are relatively free from light pollution. The festival includes stargazing events, astronomy talks, and workshops. It's a fantastic time to learn about the park's celestial wonders and enjoy the Milky Way in a pristine setting.

Bar Harbor Music Festival (July): Held in nearby Bar Harbor, this festival offers a variety of musical performances ranging from classical to jazz. It's an excellent opportunity to enjoy high-quality live music in a beautiful coastal setting. The festival runs for several weeks, featuring both established and emerging artists, and includes concerts, opera performances, and chamber music.

Mount Desert Island Marathon (October): This marathon attracts runners from around the world and offers a challenging course through some of the most scenic parts of the island. Whether you're a participant or a spectator, the event adds excitement and energy to the fall season. The marathon route includes stunning views of the coastline and the vibrant fall foliage, making it one of the most picturesque marathons in the United States.

Fourth of July Celebrations: Bar Harbor hosts one of the best Fourth of July celebrations in the region, with a parade, seafood festival, and fireworks display. It's a lively time to visit and experience local culture and festivities. The celebrations also include live music, craft fairs, and various family-friendly activities, creating a festive atmosphere that showcases the community spirit of the area.

Fall Foliage Festival (October): This festival celebrates the peak of fall colors in Acadia and includes craft fairs, local food, and live entertainment. It's a great way to experience the local community and the stunning autumn scenery. The festival is held in Bar Harbor and surrounding towns, featuring activities such as hayrides, pumpkin carving, and guided foliage tours.

Winter Holiday Events: During the winter season, Bar Harbor and other nearby towns host holiday events, including festive light displays, holiday markets, and special performances. These events add a touch of seasonal magic to a winter visit. Highlights include the annual Christmas by the Sea Festival, which features parades, tree lighting ceremonies, and visits from Santa Claus.

Best Times for Specific Activities

Hiking: The best times for hiking are late spring through fall. Early summer offers lush green landscapes, while fall provides cooler temperatures and breathtaking foliage. Trails are generally clear and accessible, although spring can be muddy, and fall may bring early snow at higher elevations. Popular hikes include the Precipice Trail, Beehive Trail, and the Cadillac Mountain South Ridge Trail.

Biking: Summer and early fall are ideal for biking, especially on the Carriage Roads. The warm weather and long daylight hours provide perfect conditions for exploring these scenic, motor-free pathways. Fall adds the bonus of colorful foliage, making it an exceptionally beautiful time to bike. The Carriage Roads, designed by John D. Rockefeller Jr., offer a network of 45 miles of gravel paths that are perfect for cyclists of all skill levels.

Water Activities: Kayaking, canoeing, and swimming are best enjoyed in the summer when water temperatures are more comfortable. Jordan Pond and Echo Lake are popular spots for kayaking, while Sand Beach offers a unique ocean swimming experience. Kayaking tours are available and provide opportunities to explore the coastline and see marine wildlife up close.

Wildlife Watching: Spring and fall are prime times for wildlife watching. In spring, migratory birds return, and many animals are more active. Fall offers opportunities to see animals preparing for winter. Early morning and late evening are generally the best times to spot wildlife. Acadia is home to a variety of species, including white-tailed deer, beavers, foxes, and numerous bird species.

Photography: Each season offers unique photographic opportunities. Spring provides vibrant wildflowers and fresh greenery, summer brings lush landscapes and clear skies, fall offers stunning foliage, and winter showcases a serene, snowy landscape. Sunrise and sunset are particularly magical times for photography, with soft lighting and dramatic colors. Cadillac Mountain is a popular spot for sunrise photography, offering panoramic views of the surrounding area.

Stargazing: While stargazing can be done year-round, the fall and winter months tend to offer the clearest skies. The Acadia Night Sky Festival in September is an excellent time to visit for astronomy enthusiasts. Winter provides particularly good conditions for stargazing due to the longer nights and minimal light pollution.

Fishing: Fishing in Acadia is best in the spring and summer months. The park's lakes and streams are home to species like brook trout and landlocked salmon. Be sure to check local regulations and obtain the necessary permits. Popular fishing spots include Eagle Lake, Jordan Pond, and Bubble Pond.

Snow Sports: Winter is the time for cross-country skiing, snowshoeing, and winter hiking. The Carriage Roads provide groomed trails for skiing, and many hiking trails are accessible for snowshoeing, offering a different perspective on the park's beauty. Winter sports equipment can be rented in Bar Harbor, and guided tours are available for those new to winter activities.

The best time to visit Acadia National Park depends on your interests and the type of experience you seek. Each season offers its own set of activities and highlights, ensuring that whenever you choose to visit, Acadia will provide a memorable and rewarding experience. Whether you're drawn by the vibrant colors of fall, the tranquil snowscapes of winter, the blossoming life of spring, or the bustling energy of summer, Acadia National Park has something special to offer.

Chapter 3: Budgeting for Your Trip

Cost Breakdown

Planning a trip to Acadia National Park involves considering various expenses to ensure a budget-friendly vacation. Here's a breakdown of the primary costs you can expect:

Transportation: Your transportation costs will depend on your starting point and the mode of transport you choose. If you're flying, the nearest major airport is Bangor International Airport (BGR), approximately 50 miles from the park. Flights can range from $200 to $500 round trip, depending on the season and departure city. From the airport, you might rent a car, which typically costs $40 to $70 per day. If driving from nearby states, factor in gas costs, which can vary but average around $3 to $4 per gallon.

Accommodation: Accommodation prices vary significantly based on location, season, and type. Campgrounds within the park, such as Blackwoods and Seawall, charge about $22 to $30 per night. Mid-range hotels and motels in Bar Harbor, the closest town to the park, typically range from $100 to $250 per night during peak season. Vacation rentals or budget motels can be found for $70 to $150 per night, especially if booked well in advance.

Food: Dining expenses depend on whether you cook your own meals or eat out. Groceries for a week can cost around $50 to $100 per person. Dining out in Bar Harbor ranges from $10 to $20 per meal at casual spots to $30 and up at nicer restaurants. Packing snacks and picnic supplies can further reduce costs.

Park Fees: Entrance to Acadia National Park requires a pass. The weekly pass is $30 per vehicle, $25 for motorcycles, and $15 for individuals on foot or bicycle. An annual pass is $55 and is a great deal if you plan multiple visits.

Activities: While many park activities are free, such as hiking and beach access, some may incur costs. Renting bikes for the Carriage Roads can cost about $30 to $50 per day. Guided tours or ranger-led programs may also have fees, generally around $10 to $25 per person.

Money-Saving Tips

Travel Off-Season: Visiting during the shoulder seasons (spring and fall) can significantly reduce costs. Accommodation rates are lower, and there are fewer crowds, which enhances the experience.

Book in Advance: Whether it's flights, car rentals, or accommodation, booking early often secures better rates. Many campgrounds in Acadia allow reservations up to six months in advance.

Use a Park Pass: If you plan to visit multiple national parks within a year, consider America the Beautiful Pass. At $80 annually, it grants access to over 2,000 federal recreation sites, including Acadia.

Pack Your Own Food: Grocery shopping and preparing your own meals can save a considerable amount of money compared to dining out for every meal. Many accommodations offer kitchenettes or allow the use of camp stoves.

Take Advantage of Free Activities: Acadia National Park offers numerous free activities such as hiking, wildlife watching, and visiting scenic overlooks. Utilize these to keep your entertainment budget low.

Share Costs: Traveling with friends or family can help divide costs like accommodation, gas, and park fees, making the trip more affordable for everyone.

Affordable Accommodation and Dining Options

Campgrounds: Staying at one of Acadia's campgrounds, like Blackwoods, Seawall, or Schoodic Woods, is one of the most budget-friendly options. These campgrounds provide basic amenities and a close connection to nature at around $22 to $30 per night.

Budget Motels and Inns: In Bar Harbor and surrounding areas, several motels and inns offer affordable lodging. Options like Edenbrook Motel, Bar Harbor Villager Motel, and High Seas Motel provide clean, comfortable rooms for $70 to $150 per night.

Vacation Rentals: Platforms like Airbnb and VRBO have numerous listings in the Acadia region. Renting a cabin or apartment can be economical, especially for families or groups. Prices range from $100 to $200 per night, depending on size and location.

Dining on a Budget: For affordable meals, look for casual dining spots in Bar Harbor such as Rosalie's Pizza, Side Street Cafe, and Jordan's Restaurant. These places offer good food at reasonable prices, with meals typically costing between $10 and $20.

Grocery Stores: Shopping at local grocery stores like Hannaford or Shaws can save money on meals. Preparing sandwiches and snacks for hikes or picnics allows you to enjoy the park's natural settings while keeping costs down.

Free and Low-Cost Activities

Hiking: With over 120 miles of hiking trails, Acadia offers routes for all skill levels, from easy strolls to challenging climbs. Popular trails like Cadillac Mountain, Jordan Pond Path, and Beehive Trail are free and provide stunning views.

Wildlife Watching: Acadia is home to diverse wildlife, including moose, black bears, and a variety of birds. Bring binoculars and enjoy wildlife watching along trails and at quiet spots like Sieur de Monts Spring and Schoodic Point.

Biking: The park's 45 miles of Carriage Roads are perfect for biking. While renting a bike incurs a fee, bringing your own bike makes this a free activity. The Carriage Roads offer scenic, car-free paths ideal for exploring the park's interior.

Beachcombing: Sand Beach and Echo Lake Beach are great spots for relaxing and beachcombing. These areas are free to access and provide a peaceful way to enjoy the park's coastal beauty.

Ranger Programs: Acadia offers various ranger-led programs, including guided hikes, stargazing events, and educational talks. Many of these programs are free or require a nominal fee, providing informative and engaging ways to learn about the park.

Picnicking: Acadia has numerous scenic picnic spots. Packing a picnic lunch and enjoying it at places like Eagle Lake or along the Park Loop Road is a cost-effective way to dine amidst stunning scenery.

Photography: Whether you're an amateur or a pro, Acadia's landscapes provide endless opportunities for photography. Sunrise at Cadillac Mountain, sunset at Bass Harbor Head Light, and the rugged coastline offer iconic scenes to capture.

Visitor Centers: The Hulls Cove Visitor Center and other information hubs within the park offer free exhibits and educational displays about

Acadia's natural and cultural history. It's a great way to learn more about the park without spending money.

By carefully planning and taking advantage of these money-saving tips, affordable accommodations, dining options, and free activities, you can enjoy a budget-friendly trip to Acadia National Park without compromising on the experience.

Chapter 4: Essentials for Traveling

Packing List

When preparing for a trip to Acadia National Park, having a comprehensive packing list ensures you are well-equipped for the diverse range of activities and weather conditions you might encounter. Here's a detailed list to help you pack effectively:

Clothing:

- Layered Clothing: The weather in Acadia can be unpredictable, so pack layers that you can add or remove as needed. Include base layers, mid-layers (like fleece or down jackets), and waterproof outer layers.
- Hiking Gear: Comfortable, moisture-wicking clothing, including hiking pants, shirts, and socks. A lightweight, long-sleeved shirt for sun protection and warmth is also useful.

- Footwear: Sturdy hiking boots with good ankle support are essential for tackling the park's rugged trails. Bring water shoes or sandals for beach and water activities.
- Rain Gear: A waterproof jacket and pants are crucial, as coastal weather can be wet and unpredictable.
- Casual Wear: Comfortable clothing for lounging around your accommodation or exploring nearby towns.
- Swimwear: For swimming at Sand Beach or Echo Lake.
- Accessories: Hats, sunglasses, and gloves (especially in cooler months).

Camping Gear (if applicable):

- Tent and Sleeping Bag: Choose a tent suitable for the season and a sleeping bag rated for the temperatures you'll encounter.
- Sleeping Pad: For added comfort and insulation from the ground.

- Camp Stove and Cooking Equipment plan to cook your own meals.
- Cooler: For storing perishables.
- Lanterns and Headlamps: For lighting your campsite at night.
- Camping Chair: For comfortable seating around the campfire.

Personal Items:

- Toiletries: Including biodegradable soap, toothbrush, toothpaste, and other personal hygiene items.
- Sunscreen and Insect Repellent: To protect against sunburn and bug bites.
- First Aid Kit: Including bandages, antiseptic wipes, pain relievers, and any personal medications.
- Water Bottles and Hydration System: Staying hydrated is crucial, especially during long hikes.

- Maps and Guidebooks: Physical maps and guidebooks can be invaluable, especially in areas with limited cell service.
- Binoculars and Camera: For wildlife watching and capturing scenic views.

Miscellaneous:
- Backpack: A daypack for hikes to carry water, snacks, and essentials.
- Trekking Poles: Helpful for stability on uneven terrain.
- Multi-tool or Pocket Knife: Useful for a variety of tasks.
- Chargers and Power Banks: For keeping electronic devices charged.
- Trash Bags: Leave no trace by packing out all your waste.

Health and Safety Tips

Staying healthy and safe during your visit to Acadia National Park involves a combination of preparation, awareness, and adhering to guidelines. Here are some key health and safety tips:

- Stay Hydrated: Always carry enough water, especially during hikes. Dehydration can occur quickly, particularly in warm weather or during strenuous activities.
- Weather Preparedness: Acadia's weather can change rapidly. Dress in layers, carry rain gear, and check weather forecasts before heading out. Avoid exposed areas during thunderstorms.
- Trail Safety: Stick to marked trails and respect trail closures. Inform someone of your itinerary, and carry a map, compass, or GPS device. Be aware of your physical limits and avoid overly strenuous hikes.
- Wildlife Awareness: Maintain a safe distance from wildlife and never feed animals. Familiarize yourself with the local fauna and

how to respond to encounters, particularly with larger animals like moose or black bears.
- Sun Protection: Use sunscreen, wear a hat, and sunglasses to protect yourself from UV radiation. Even on cloudy days, UV exposure can be significant.
- Insect Protection: Use insect repellent and wear long sleeves and pants to prevent bites from mosquitoes and ticks, which can carry diseases.
- Emergency Preparedness: Carry a basic first aid kit and know how to use it. Familiarize yourself with the locations of the nearest medical facilities and ranger stations.
- Leave No Trace: Follow the principles of Leave No Trace to minimize your impact on the environment. This includes packing out all trash, staying on designated trails, and respecting wildlife and other visitors.
- Water Safety: Exercise caution when engaging in water activities. Wear life jackets

when boating or kayaking, and be aware of strong currents and cold water temperatures.

Travel Insurance

Travel insurance is a crucial consideration for any trip, including a visit to Acadia National Park. Here's why it's important and what to look for:

Why You Need Travel Insurance:
- Medical Coverage: Covers medical expenses in case of illness or injury. This is especially important if you plan to engage in outdoor activities that carry a risk of injury.
- Trip Cancellation/Interruption: Protect your investment if you need to cancel or cut short your trip due to unforeseen circumstances, such as family emergencies or severe weather.

- Lost or Stolen Belongings: Reimburses you for lost, stolen, or damaged luggage and personal items.
- Emergency Evacuation: Covers costs associated with emergency transportation in case of severe injury or illness.

What to Look For:
- Coverage Limits: Ensure the policy has sufficient coverage for medical expenses and emergency evacuation.
- Adventure Activities: Verify that the policy covers the specific activities you plan to do, such as hiking, kayaking, or biking.
- Trip Duration: Confirm that the policy duration covers your entire trip.
- Exclusions and Conditions: Read the fine print to understand what is not covered and any conditions that must be met for a claim.

Recommended Providers:

- World Nomads: Known for covering a wide range of adventure activities.
- Allianz Global Assistance: Offers comprehensive plans with high coverage limits.
- Travel Guard: Provides customizable plans with various coverage options.

Communication and Connectivity

Staying connected during your visit to Acadia National Park can be challenging due to the park's remote location and rugged terrain. Here are some tips for maintaining communication and connectivity:

- Cell Phone Coverage: Cell phone service can be spotty in Acadia, particularly in more remote areas. Major carriers like Verizon and AT&T generally have the best coverage.

Before you go, check your carrier's coverage map and inform others that you may be out of reach.

- Wi-Fi Access: Wi-Fi is available at some visitor centers, lodges, and cafes in nearby towns like Bar Harbor. However, it may not be reliable for high-speed needs. Plan to download maps, guidebooks, and other essential information before entering the park.

- Two-Way Radios: Consider bringing two-way radios for communication, especially if you're traveling in a group and plan to split up. These can be invaluable in areas with no cell service.

- Portable Chargers and Power Banks: Leep your devices charged with portable chargers and power banks, as charging opportunities may be limited. Solar chargers can be a good option for longer trips.

- Emergency Communication Devices: For remote areas, consider renting or purchasing a satellite phone or a personal locator beacon (PLB). These devices can send emergency signals and communicate in areas without cell service.

- Apps and Offline Maps: Download offline maps from apps like AllTrails or Gaia GPS. These can help you navigate the trails even without cell service.

- Informing Others: Always inform someone of your itinerary and expected return times. This ensures someone knows your whereabouts in case of an emergency.

By following these guidelines and being well-prepared, you can ensure a safe, enjoyable, and well-connected trip to Acadia National Park. Proper packing, health and safety measures, travel insurance, and reliable communication methods will enhance your travel experience and provide peace of mind throughout your adventure.

Chapter 5: Entry and Visa Requirements

Visa Information for International Visitors

International visitors planning a trip to Acadia National Park in the United States must navigate the visa and entry requirements set by U.S. immigration authorities. Here is an overview of the process and key information to ensure a smooth entry into the country.

Visa Waiver Program (VWP): Citizens of 40 countries, including most European nations, Australia, Japan, and South Korea, can travel to the U.S. for tourism or business for up to 90 days without a visa under the Visa Waiver Program. Visitors must apply for authorization through the Electronic System for Travel Authorization (ESTA) before traveling. ESTA approval usually takes a few minutes but can take up to 72 hours, so it's advisable to apply well in advance.

Tourist Visa (B-2): Visitors from countries not included in the VWP need to apply for a B-2 Tourist Visa. This process involves completing the DS-160 form, paying a visa application fee, and scheduling an interview at a U.S. embassy or consulate. During the interview, applicants should be prepared to demonstrate ties to their home country, such as employment, family, and property, to prove their intent to return after their trip.

Visa Application Process:
- Complete the DS-160 Form: This is an online form available on the U.S. Department of State's website. It requires detailed information about your travel plans and background.
- Pay the Application Fee: The fee for a B-2 visa is currently $160, but it's essential to check the latest fee as it can change.

- Schedule an Interview: Interviews are required for most applicants. Exceptions include those under 14 or over 79 years of age. Wait times for interviews vary, so it's advisable to schedule early.
- Prepare for the Interview: Bring required documents, including your passport (valid for at least six months beyond your planned stay), a recent photograph, confirmation of your DS-160 form, and proof of payment. Additional documents, such as a travel itinerary, evidence of financial support, and ties to your home country, can strengthen your application.

Upon Arrival:
- Customs and Border Protection (CBP): Upon arrival in the U.S., visitors will go through CBP inspection. Have your passport, visa, and travel documents ready. Be prepared to answer questions about your trip purpose and duration.

- I-94 Form: Visitors will be issued an I-94 form, which records entry and exit dates. This can be accessed online and should be checked for accuracy.

Park Entry Fees and Passes

Acadia National Park, like many U.S. national parks, charges an entry fee that contributes to park maintenance and visitor services. Understanding the fee structure and available passes can help you plan and budget your visit effectively.

Standard Entrance Fees:
- Private Vehicle: A seven-day pass for a private vehicle costs $30. This pass covers all occupants of the vehicle.
- Motorcycle: The fee for a motorcycle is $25 for a seven-day pass.

- Individual (on foot or bicycle): Individuals entering the park without a vehicle pay $15 each for a seven-day pass.

Annual Passes:

- Acadia Annual Pass: For $55, this pass provides unlimited entry to Acadia National Park for one year from the month of purchase.
- America the Beautiful Pass: This $80 pass grants access to over 2,000 federal recreation sites, including all national parks, for one year. It covers entrance fees for the pass holder and accompanying passengers in a single, non-commercial vehicle.

Special Passes:

- Senior Pass: U.S. citizens or permanent residents aged 62 and older can purchase a lifetime Senior Pass for $80 or an annual pass for $20. This pass provides the same benefits as the America the Beautiful Pass.

- Military Pass: Active-duty military members and their dependents are eligible for a free annual pass. Proper identification is required.
- Access Pass: U.S. citizens or permanent residents with permanent disabilities can obtain a free lifetime Access Pass, which includes the same benefits as other annual passes.

Purchase Locations:
- Online: Passes can be purchased in advance through the National Park Service website or other authorized vendors.
- In-Person: Passes are available at park entrance stations and visitor centers.

Registration and Permits for Specific Activities

While many activities in Acadia National Park can be enjoyed with just the standard entry pass, some require additional permits and registration. Understanding these requirements ensures compliance with park regulations and enhances your experience.

Camping:

- Reservation Required: All campgrounds in Acadia National Park require reservations. Popular campgrounds like Blackwoods,

Seawall, and Schoodic Woods fill up quickly, so it's advisable to book several months in advance. Reservations can be made through Recreation.gov.
- Fees: Camping fees range from $22 to $30 per night, depending on the campground and season.
- Backcountry Camping: Acadia does not offer traditional backcountry camping, but it's important to respect designated camping areas to protect the park's natural resources.

Group Camping:

- Special Permits: Groups of more than 15 people require a special use permit for camping. Contact the park's permit office for details and application procedures.

Rock Climbing and Bouldering:

- Registration: While not always mandatory, climbers are encouraged to register at visitor centers for safety purposes. This helps park

rangers know the locations of climbers in case of emergencies.
- Guidelines: Follow Leave No Trace principles, use established climbing routes, and avoid areas with nesting birds or other wildlife.

Boating and Kayaking:
- Permits: Non-motorized boats do not require a permit, but motorized boats must comply with Maine state boating regulations. Registration and proof of a safety course may be required for motorized boats.
- Access Points: Popular launch points include Bar Harbor, Seal Cove, and Northeast Harbor.

Fishing:
- License Required: A valid Maine fishing license is required for fishing within the park. Licenses can be purchased online or at local retailers.

- Regulations: Follow state regulations regarding catch limits, seasons, and species. Special rules may apply in certain park areas.

Special Use Permits:
- Events and Commercial Activities: Weddings, commercial filming, and other special events require a permit. Application processes and fees vary based on the activity. Contact the park's permit office well in advance to secure approval.

Ranger-Led Programs and Tours:
- Registration: Some ranger-led programs and tours may require advance registration due to limited space. Check the park's website or visitor centers for schedules and registration details.

Trail Use:
- Group Hikes: Large groups should inform park rangers of their plans to ensure trail

capacity and safety. Some trails may have group size limits to protect the environment and ensure a pleasant experience for all visitors.

Winter Activities:

- Snowmobiling: Snowmobiles are allowed on designated roads and areas within the park. A Maine snowmobile registration is required.
- Cross-Country Skiing and Snowshoeing: These activities are popular on the park's Carriage Roads. No permits are required, but check trail conditions and weather reports for safety.

By understanding and adhering to these entry and visa requirements, park entry fees, and permits, international visitors and U.S. residents alike can enjoy a well-prepared and enjoyable visit to Acadia National Park. Proper planning ensures compliance with regulations, enhances the overall experience, and helps preserve the park's natural beauty for future generations.

Chapter 6: Exploring the Park

Top Hiking Trails

Acadia National Park offers an extensive network of hiking trails, providing a variety of experiences for visitors of all skill levels. Here are some of the top hiking trails that highlight the park's diverse landscapes:

1. Cadillac Mountain Summit Trail:
- Difficulty: Moderate
- Length: 3.5 miles round trip

- Description: As the highest peak on the U.S. Atlantic coast, Cadillac Mountain offers panoramic views of the park and surrounding areas. The summit trail is moderately challenging, with rocky terrain and several steep sections. The reward is a breathtaking view, especially at sunrise, when Cadillac Mountain is one of the first places in the U.S. to see the morning sun.

2. Jordan Pond Path:
- Difficulty: Easy to Moderate
- Length: 3.3 miles loop
- Description: This trail circles the serene Jordan Pond, offering stunning views of the Bubbles (two rounded hills) and the crystal-clear waters of the pond. The path is relatively flat and well-maintained, making it accessible for most hikers. It's an excellent option for families and those looking for a leisurely hike with plenty of photo opportunities.

3. Precipice Trail:
- Difficulty: Strenuous
- Length: 2.5 miles round trip
- Description: Known for its challenging ascent, the Precipice Trail is not for the faint of heart. Hikers navigate steep cliffs, iron rungs, and ladders. This trail is best suited for experienced hikers with a good head for heights. The exhilarating climb is rewarded with spectacular views of Frenchman Bay and the surrounding landscape.

4. Beehive Trail:
- Difficulty: Strenuous
- Length: 1.5 miles loop
- Description: Similar to the Precipice Trail, the Beehive Trail offers an adventurous hike with iron rungs and steep drop-offs. It's a shorter, yet equally thrilling alternative, providing impressive views over Sand Beach and the surrounding areas. Hikers should

exercise caution and be prepared for a challenging climb.

5. Ocean Path:
- Difficulty: Easy
- Length: 4.4 miles round trip
- Description: This popular coastal trail runs from Sand Beach to Otter Point, offering continuous ocean views and access to iconic landmarks such as Thunder Hole and Monument Cove. The relatively flat path is ideal for casual walkers and families, with numerous spots to stop and enjoy the scenery.

6. Gorham Mountain Trail:
- -Difficulty: Moderate
- Length: 3.2 miles round trip
- Description: This trail provides a moderate hike with rewarding views from the summit of Gorham Mountain. Hikers can enjoy panoramic vistas of the park's coastline and

islands. The trail is less crowded than some of the more popular routes, offering a peaceful hiking experience.

7. Bubble Rock Trail:
- Difficulty: Moderate
- Length: 1 mile round trip
- Description: This short but steep trail leads to the famous Bubble Rock, a glacial erratic perched precariously on the edge of South Bubble Mountain. The trail offers excellent views of Jordan Pond and the surrounding area. It's a must-visit for its unique geological features and scenic outlook.

Scenic Drives

Acadia National Park's scenic drives allow visitors to experience the park's beauty from the comfort of their vehicle. These drives offer convenient access to some of the park's most stunning vistas and landmarks.

1. Park Loop Road:
- Length: 27 miles
- Description: The Park Loop Road is the quintessential driving tour of Acadia, winding through forests, along the rugged coast, and past numerous scenic viewpoints. Key stops along the way include Cadillac Mountain, Sand Beach, Thunder Hole, and Jordan Pond. This drive is especially popular during the fall foliage season when the park's landscapes are ablaze with color.

2. Cadillac Mountain Summit Road:
- Length: 3.5 miles one way
- Description: This drive takes visitors to the summit of Cadillac Mountain, offering sweeping views of the park and beyond. The road is open from late spring to early fall, with restricted access during winter months.

Sunrise and sunset are particularly popular times to visit, though reservations may be required during peak times.

3. Schoodic Peninsula Scenic Drive:
- Length: 6-mile loop
- Description: Located on the mainland portion of Acadia, the Schoodic Peninsula offers a quieter, less-visited experience. The scenic drive around the peninsula features dramatic coastal views, crashing waves, and opportunities to spot seabirds and other wildlife. Highlights include Schoodic Point and Blueberry Hill.

4. Isle au Haut Road:
- Length: Varies
- Description: Accessible by ferry from Stonington, Isle au Haut offers a more remote and less-developed experience. The island's few roads provide access to rugged coastal trails, secluded coves, and quiet

picnic spots. Visitors should plan ahead, as services and facilities are limited.

Wildlife Watching

Acadia National Park is a haven for wildlife enthusiasts, offering diverse habitats that support a wide range of species. Here are some tips and prime locations for wildlife watching in the park:

1. Schoodic Peninsula:
- Species: Seabirds, bald eagles, harbor seals

- Description: The Schoodic Peninsula is excellent for spotting seabirds and bald eagles. The rocky shores and crashing waves create a dramatic backdrop for wildlife viewing. Harbor seals can often be seen basking on the rocks or swimming in the surf.

2. *Jordan Pond:*
   - Species: Loons, beavers, otters
   - Description: The calm waters of Jordan Pond attract a variety of waterfowl, including loons and ducks. The surrounding wetlands are home to beavers and otters, which can sometimes be seen early in the morning or late in the evening.

3. *Cadillac Mountain:*
   - Species: Peregrine falcons, songbirds, deer
   - Description: Cadillac Mountain is a great spot for birdwatching, especially during migration seasons. Peregrine falcons nest on

the cliffs, and various songbirds can be seen in the woodlands. Deer are also commonly spotted in the area.

4. Sieur de Monts Spring:
- Species: Warblers, woodpeckers, amphibians
- Description: The diverse habitats around Sieur de Monts Spring support a rich array of bird species, particularly during spring and fall migrations. The area's wetlands are also a good place to observe frogs and salamanders.

5. Seal Cove:
- Species: Seals, seabirds, ospreys
- Description: Seal Cove is aptly named for the harbor seals that frequent the area. It's also a good location for viewing seabirds and ospreys. Bring binoculars for the best experience.

Water Activities

Acadia National Park's coastal and freshwater environments provide ample opportunities for water-based activities. Whether you prefer the thrill of kayaking or the relaxation of swimming, there's something for everyone.

1. Kayaking and Canoeing:

- Locations: Bar Harbor, Jordan Pond, Long Pond
- Description: Kayaking and canoeing are popular ways to explore Acadia's waterways. Sea kayaking along the rugged coastline offers spectacular views and the chance to see marine wildlife up close. Freshwater options like Jordan Pond and Long Pond provide a more tranquil paddling experience. Rentals and guided tours are available in Bar Harbor and other nearby towns.

2. Swimming:

- Locations: Sand Beach, Echo Lake, Lake Wood
- Description: While Acadia's coastal waters can be quite cold, Sand Beach is a popular spot for swimming. For warmer water, Echo Lake and Lake Wood offer excellent freshwater swimming options. Both have designated swimming areas and are ideal for families.

3. Tidepooling:

- Locations: Wonderland, Ship Harbor, Bar Island
- Description: Exploring the intertidal zones is a fascinating activity, especially for families. At low tide, areas like Wonderland and Ship Harbor reveal a variety of marine life, including starfish, crabs, and sea anemones. Bar Island, accessible at low tide, is another great spot for tidepooling.

4. Boating and Sailing:

- Locations: Frenchman Bay, Somes Sound, Cranberry Isles
- Description: Boating and sailing offer unique perspectives of Acadia's coastline. Frenchman Bay is popular for boat tours and sailing excursions, providing opportunities to see wildlife and scenic landmarks from the water. Somes Sound, a fjard (glacially carved inlet), and the Cranberry Isles are also beautiful areas to explore by boat.

5. Fishing:

- Locations: Jordan Pond, Long Pond, Eagle Lake
- Description: Fishing is a peaceful way to enjoy Acadia's lakes and ponds. Anglers can fish for species like brook trout, landlocked salmon, and smallmouth bass. A valid Maine fishing license is required, and anglers should be aware of local regulations and catch limits.

Exploring Acadia National Park offers endless opportunities for adventure and relaxation. Whether hiking its rugged trails, driving along scenic routes, observing wildlife, or enjoying water activities, there is something for everyone to appreciate in this stunning natural wonder. Proper planning and respect for park regulations will enhance your experience and help preserve Acadia's beauty for future generations.

Chapter 7: Cultural Experiences

Local History and Traditions

Acadia National Park, situated along the rugged coastline of Maine, is steeped in rich local history and traditions that provide a deeper understanding of the area's cultural heritage. This section delves into the historical significance and traditional practices that have shaped the region.

Indigenous Heritage:

The Wabanaki people, specifically the Penobscot, Passamaquoddy, Maliseet, and Mi'kmaq tribes, are the original inhabitants of the region encompassing Acadia National Park. These tribes have a deep connection to the land, with traditions and practices that have been passed down through generations. Their legacy is evident in the place names, legends, and continued presence in the area.

European Settlement:

The history of European settlement in Acadia dates back to the early 17th century when French explorers, led by Samuel de Champlain, arrived in the region. The name "Acadia" itself is derived from the French "Arcadie," a term that evoked a pastoral utopia. The French settlers, known as Acadians, established farming and fishing communities, which were later overtaken by the British in the mid-18th century.

Maritime Traditions:

Maritime activities have been a cornerstone of life in Acadia. The region's economy historically relied on shipbuilding, fishing, and trade. These maritime traditions are celebrated through local festivals, boat-building workshops, and historical reenactments. The Maine Maritime Museum in nearby Bath offers insights into the state's rich seafaring history.

Preservation Efforts:
The establishment of Acadia National Park itself is a testament to the dedication of local residents and philanthropists like George B. Dorr, Charles W. Eliot, and John D. Rockefeller Jr. Their efforts in land conservation and the creation of carriage roads, bridges, and other infrastructure have preserved the natural and cultural heritage of the area for future generations.

Museums and Cultural Centers

Exploring the museums and cultural centers around Acadia National Park provides visitors with a deeper appreciation of the region's history, art, and natural environment. Here are some key institutions to visit:

Abbe Museum:

Located in Bar Harbor, the Abbe Museum is dedicated to the history and culture of the Wabanaki people. It offers exhibits, educational programs, and artifacts that highlight the traditions and contemporary lives of the indigenous tribes of Maine. The museum also hosts workshops, lectures, and events that foster cultural understanding and appreciation.

Sieur de Monts Spring Nature Center:

This center within Acadia National Park provides educational exhibits about the park's natural and cultural history. Visitors can learn about the flora, fauna, and geological features of the park, as well as the history of human interaction with the landscape. The nearby Wild Gardens of Acadia showcase native plant species and their ecological significance.

Maine Granite Industry Historical Society Museum:

Situated in Mount Desert, this museum chronicles the history of granite quarrying in the region. The exhibits include tools, photographs, and documents that tell the story of the industry that once played a significant role in the local economy. Visitors can learn about the quarrying process and the lives of the workers who contributed to this important industry.

Bar Harbor Historical Society Museum:

Housed in the former St. Edward's Convent, this museum offers exhibits on the history of Bar Harbor and Mount Desert Island. It features artifacts, photographs, and documents that highlight the area's development, from its early settlement to its rise as a premier tourist destination. The museum also explores the impact of significant events, such as the Great Fire of 1947.

Local Cuisine and Dining Experiences

Experiencing the local cuisine is an integral part of any visit to Acadia National Park. The region offers a variety of dining options that showcase the flavors of Maine, particularly its renowned seafood.

Seafood Specialties:

Maine is famous for its seafood, and no visit to Acadia is complete without indulging in some local favorites. Lobster is a must-try, whether you enjoy it in a traditional lobster roll, steamed with butter, or in a classic lobster bake. Other seafood delicacies include fresh clams, mussels, scallops, and Atlantic salmon.

Farm-to-Table Dining:

The farm-to-table movement is strong in the region, with many restaurants sourcing their ingredients from local farms and fisheries. This commitment to fresh, locally sourced produce ensures that diners enjoy the best flavors of the season. Restaurants like Cafe This Way in Bar Harbor and Red Sky in Southwest Harbor are known for their creative use of local ingredients.

Blueberry Delights:
Maine is also famous for its wild blueberries, which are smaller and more flavorful than their cultivated counterparts. These blueberries find their way into a variety of dishes, from pancakes and muffins to pies and jams. Be sure to try a slice of blueberry pie, often served à la mode with a scoop of vanilla ice cream.

Craft Breweries and Distilleries:
The craft beverage scene in Maine is thriving, with numerous breweries and distilleries offering unique local brews and spirits. Bar Harbor's Atlantic Brewing Company and Mount Desert Island's Mainely Meat BBQ & Brews are popular spots to sample locally crafted beers. For spirits, the

Sweetgrass Farm Winery and Distillery offers tours and tastings of their handcrafted gin, rum, and other spirits.

Art and Craft Markets

The artistic spirit of Acadia National Park and its surrounding communities is reflected in the numerous art and craft markets, where visitors can find unique, locally made items. These markets offer a chance to meet local artisans and purchase one-of-a-kind souvenirs.

Island Artisans:
This cooperative gallery in Bar Harbor features the work of over 30 local artists. Visitors can browse a wide range of handmade items, including pottery, jewelry, textiles, woodwork, and paintings. The gallery is a great place to find high-quality, unique pieces that capture the essence of Acadia.

Seal Harbor Artisans Market:

Held seasonally in the charming village of Seal Harbor, this market showcases the talents of local artists and craftsmen. Items for sale include handmade jewelry, knitted goods, paintings, and photography. The market provides an intimate setting to meet the artists and learn about their creative processes.

Acadia Arts and Crafts:

Located in Southwest Harbor, this shop offers a curated selection of handmade goods from local artisans. The inventory includes ceramics, glassware, metalwork, and fine art. It's an excellent place to find a special memento of your trip to Acadia.

Bar Harbor Summer Arts and Crafts Fair:

This annual event, typically held in July, brings together a diverse group of artists and craftspeople. The fair features a wide array of handmade products, from fine art and photography to jewelry and woodworking. Live music and food vendors add to the festive atmosphere, making it a fun outing for the whole family.

Exploring the cultural experiences in and around Acadia National Park enriches your visit, providing insights into the local history, traditions, and artistic expressions that define this unique region. Whether delving into the past at a museum, savoring local cuisine, or discovering handmade treasures, these experiences offer a deeper connection to the spirit of Acadia.

Chapter 8: Family-Friendly Activities

Kid-Friendly Hikes and Trails

Acadia National Park offers numerous trails and outdoor experiences perfect for families with children. These kid-friendly hikes are designed to be enjoyable, educational, and safe for young adventurers.

1. Wonderland Trail:
- Difficulty: Easy
- Length: 1.4 miles round trip
- Description: The Wonderland Trail is a flat, easy hike through a coastal forest that leads to a rocky shoreline. It's perfect for families with young children, offering plenty of opportunities to explore tide pools, collect seashells, and spot wildlife. The trail is wide

and well-maintained, making it accessible for strollers and small children.

2. *Ship Harbor Nature Trail:*
- Difficulty: Easy
- Length: 1.3 miles loop
- Description: This loop trail provides a gentle walk through forests and along the coast. Interpretive signs along the way educate hikers about the local ecosystem and geology. The Ship Harbor Nature Trail is great for curious kids who enjoy learning about their surroundings. The varied terrain keeps the hike interesting without being too challenging.

3. *Jordan Pond Path:*
- Difficulty: Easy to Moderate
- Length: 3.3 miles loop
- Description: While a bit longer, the Jordan Pond Path is mostly flat and well-suited for families. The trail encircles Jordan Pond,

offering stunning views of the Bubbles and the clear waters of the pond. Families can enjoy a leisurely walk, and there are plenty of spots to rest and enjoy a picnic. After the hike, the Jordan Pond House is a great place to stop for popovers and tea.

4. Bubble Rock Trail:
- Difficulty: Moderate
- Length: 1 mile round trip
- Description: The Bubble Rock Trail is a short but moderately steep hike leading to a large glacial erratic perched on the edge of South Bubble Mountain. The sight of Bubble Rock precariously balanced is a hit with kids, and the views of Jordan Pond from the top are spectacular. The trail is manageable for school-aged children who enjoy a bit of a climb.

5. Great Head Trail:
- Difficulty: Moderate

- Length: 1.4 miles loop
- Description: Starting from Sand Beach, the Great Head Trail offers a bit of everything—beach, forest, and rocky cliffs. The trail is relatively short but provides varied scenery and a bit of adventure for older kids. The climb up to Great Head offers rewarding views of the coastline and Frenchman Bay.

Educational Programs and Junior Ranger Activities

Acadia National Park is committed to providing educational opportunities for young visitors. Through various programs and activities, children can learn about the park's natural and cultural history while having fun.

Junior Ranger Program:

The Junior Ranger Program is a fantastic way for kids to engage with the park. Upon arrival, children can pick up a Junior Ranger booklet at any visitor center. The booklet contains activities and questions that encourage kids to explore and learn about different aspects of the park. Completing the booklet earns them an official Junior Ranger badge, a proud accomplishment for young explorers.

Ranger-Led Programs:

Throughout the year, Acadia offers ranger-led programs tailored to different age groups. These programs include nature walks, wildlife talks, and hands-on activities that teach children about the park's flora, fauna, and geology. These interactive sessions are both educational and entertaining, making learning about the park a fun family activity.

Nature Centers and Exhibits:

The Sieur de Monts Nature Center and the Schoodic Education and Research Center provide excellent opportunities for kids to learn about the park's ecosystems and conservation efforts. Interactive exhibits, touch tanks, and educational displays make these centers a hit with children. They can learn about everything from tidal pools to the history of the park's creation.

Children's Storytime:

During the summer, many libraries and community centers around Acadia host children's storytime sessions featuring books about nature and wildlife. These story sessions often include craft activities related to the themes of the books, providing a fun, indoor break from outdoor adventures.

Best Picnic Spots and Play Areas

Acadia National Park is dotted with scenic picnic spots and areas where families can relax and enjoy the natural beauty. These locations are ideal for a meal or a rest during a day of exploring.

1. Jordan Pond House Lawn:
- Description: The lawn at Jordan Pond House is a picturesque spot for a family picnic. With views of Jordan Pond and the Bubbles, it's a perfect place to relax and enjoy the famous popovers and tea from the nearby Jordan Pond House. Kids can run and play on the expansive lawn while parents enjoy the stunning scenery.

2. Echo Lake Beach:
- Description: Echo Lake Beach is one of the best places for a family picnic. The sandy beach is perfect for swimming and playing in the water, and there are picnic tables and grills available for use. The calm, warmer waters of Echo Lake make it a favorite spot for families with young children.

3. Seawall Picnic Area:

- Description: Located near the Seawall Campground, this picnic area offers tables and grills with a beautiful oceanfront setting. The rocky shoreline provides a unique landscape for kids to explore tide pools and look for marine life. It's a quiet and less crowded spot, ideal for a peaceful family picnic.

4. Thompson Island Picnic Area:

- Description: This picnic area, located at the entrance to Mount Desert Island, offers a scenic spot with views of the water and surrounding islands. It's equipped with picnic tables, grills, and restrooms, making it convenient for families. The location is great for a quick stop before or after exploring the park.

5. Cadillac Mountain Summit:

- Description: For a picnic with a view, the summit of Cadillac Mountain is unparalleled. While there are no picnic tables, families can spread out a blanket and enjoy their meal with panoramic views of the park and beyond. This spot is particularly popular at sunrise and sunset, offering a breathtaking backdrop for a memorable family picnic.

Exploring Acadia National Park as a family provides endless opportunities for adventure, learning, and quality time together. Whether hiking kid-friendly trails, participating in educational programs, or enjoying a picnic in a scenic spot, there's something for every member of the family to enjoy. The park's natural beauty and family-friendly amenities make it an ideal destination for creating lasting memories.

Chapter 9: Acadia National Park Accommodations

Luxury Hotels

1. The Claremont Hotel
- Price: Starting from $450 per night
- Location: 22 Claremont Road, Southwest Harbor, ME 04679
- Booking Phone Contact: (207) 244-5036
- Description: Nestled in the charming village of Southwest Harbor, The Claremont Hotel offers an exquisite retreat with stunning views of Somes Sound. This historic hotel features beautifully appointed rooms, fine dining, and a relaxing spa, making it an ideal choice for those seeking luxury and tranquility.

2. Harborside Hotel, Spa & Marina

- Price: Starting from $400 per night
- Location: 55 West Street, Bar Harbor, ME 04609
- Booking Phone Contact: (207) 288-5033
- Description: Located in the heart of Bar Harbor, Harborside Hotel, Spa & Marina provides guests with top-notch amenities, including a full-service spa, waterfront dining, and easy access to downtown attractions. The hotel's luxurious rooms and suites offer stunning views of Frenchman Bay, ensuring a memorable stay.

3. West Street Hotel

- Price: Starting from $375 per night
- Location: 50 West Street, Bar Harbor, ME 04609
- Booking Phone Contact: (207) 288-0825
- Description: The West Street Hotel offers a blend of modern elegance and traditional charm. With its prime location overlooking the harbor, guests can enjoy upscale

accommodations, an on-site restaurant, and a rooftop pool with panoramic views of the bay and Acadia National Park.

Budget-Friendly Hotels

1. Anchorage Motel
- Price: Starting from $120 per night
- Location: 51 Mount Desert Street, Bar Harbor, ME 04609
- Booking Phone Contact: (207) 288-3959
- Description: The Anchorage Motel offers clean and comfortable accommodations at an affordable price. Conveniently located within walking distance to downtown Bar Harbor, this motel is an excellent choice for budget-conscious travelers looking to explore Acadia National Park.

2. Bar Harbor Motel
- Price: Starting from $130 per night

- Location: 100 Eden Street, Bar Harbor, ME 04609
- Booking Phone Contact: (207) 288-3453
- Description: The Bar Harbor Motel provides budget-friendly lodging with easy access to Acadia National Park and the village of Bar Harbor. Guests can enjoy spacious rooms, complimentary breakfast, and a seasonal outdoor pool, all within a short drive to the park's entrance.

3. Edenbrook Motel

- Price: Starting from $110 per night
- Location: 96 Eden Street, Bar Harbor, ME 04609
- Booking Phone Contact: (207) 288-5823
- Description: Edenbrook Motel is a great option for travelers seeking economical accommodations without sacrificing convenience. Located near the park and downtown Bar Harbor, this motel offers

comfortable rooms and a friendly atmosphere.

Restaurants

1. Jordan Pond House Restaurant
- Location: Park Loop Road, Seal Harbor, ME 04675
- Description: Famous for its popovers and tea, Jordan Pond House Restaurant offers a unique dining experience with stunning views of Jordan Pond and the Bubbles. The menu features a variety of local seafood, fresh salads, and hearty entrees, making it a must-visit spot in Acadia National Park.

2. Cafe This Way
- Location: 14 Mount Desert Street, Bar Harbor, ME 04609
- Description: Cafe This Way is a beloved local eatery known for its eclectic menu and cozy

atmosphere. Serving breakfast, lunch, and dinner, the restaurant offers a diverse range of dishes, from classic American fare to creative international cuisine.

3. Side Street Cafe

- Location: 49 Rodick Street, Bar Harbor, ME 04609
- Description: Side Street Cafe is a popular spot for both locals and visitors, offering a relaxed dining experience with a menu full of delicious options. From lobster rolls and clam chowder to vegetarian dishes and craft cocktails, there's something for everyone to enjoy.

Chapter 10: 5-Day Itinerary for Acadia National Park

Day 1: Arrival & Exploration

Morning
- Arrive in Bar Harbor and check into your chosen hotel.
- Enjoy a leisurely breakfast at Cafe This Way.

Afternoon
- Head to the Hulls Cove Visitor Center to gather information and maps for your visit.
- Drive along the scenic Park Loop Road, stopping at popular spots like Sand Beach and Thunder Hole.

Evening

- Dinner at Jordan Pond House Restaurant. Enjoy the famous popovers with a view of Jordan Pond.
- Return to your hotel and relax after your day of travel.

Day 2: Hiking and Sightseeing

Morning
- Early breakfast at your hotel or a nearby cafe.
- Hike the Cadillac Mountain Summit Trail for breathtaking views of the sunrise over the park.

Afternoon
- Picnic lunch at Jordan Pond.
- Explore the Carriage Roads on foot or by renting a bike. Stop at the iconic stone bridges and enjoy the tranquil scenery.

Evening
- Dinner at Side Street Cafe. Try their lobster roll and relax in the casual atmosphere.
- Stroll through downtown Bar Harbor and visit local shops and galleries.

Day 3: Wildlife and Water Activities

Morning
- Breakfast at Cafe This Way.
- Take a whale-watching tour from Bar Harbor. Keep an eye out for humpback whales, puffins, and other marine wildlife.

Afternoon
- Lunch at a waterfront restaurant in Bar Harbor.
- Rent kayaks or canoes and paddle along the shores of Echo Lake or Long Pond.

Evening
- Return to Bar Harbor for dinner at a local seafood restaurant.
- Enjoy a sunset cruise around Frenchman Bay for stunning views and photo opportunities.

Day 4: Cultural and Historical Sites

Morning
- Breakfast at your hotel or a local cafe.
- Visit the Abbe Museum in Bar Harbor to learn about the history and culture of the Wabanaki people.

Afternoon
- Lunch at Jordan Pond House Restaurant.

- Explore the Sieur de Monts Spring area, including the Nature Center, Wild Gardens of Acadia, and the historic Spring House.

Evening
- Dinner at Side Street Cafe.
- Attend a ranger-led program or campfire talk in the park to learn more about Acadia's natural and cultural history.

Day 5: Relaxation and Departure

Morning
- Breakfast at Cafe This Way.
- Take a leisurely walk along the **Ocean Path Trail, enjoying the coastal views and fresh sea air.

Afternoon

- Lunch at a local cafe or restaurant in Bar Harbor.
- Spend your final hours in the park visiting any spots you missed or relaxing at Sand Beach.

Evening

- Early dinner at a Bar Harbor restaurant before heading back to your hotel.
- Check out of your hotel and depart, taking with you memories of a wonderful trip to Acadia National Park.

Chapter 11: Sustainable Travel Tips

Leave No Trace Principles

When visiting natural areas like Acadia National Park, it's essential to minimize your environmental impact. The Leave No Trace (LNT) principles provide a set of guidelines to help visitors protect and preserve the natural environment. Here are the seven core principles and how they apply to Acadia:

1. Plan Ahead and Prepare:
- Research the park's regulations and guidelines before your trip. Knowing what to expect can help you avoid unexpected issues and reduce your impact. For example, certain areas may be off-limits to protect wildlife habitats.
- Prepare for the weather and terrain by packing appropriate gear and supplies. This

includes maps, first aid kits, and adequate clothing to prevent getting lost or injured.

2. Travel and Camp on Durable Surfaces:
- Stick to established trails and campsites to avoid damaging fragile ecosystems. Wandering off-trail can lead to soil erosion and harm vegetation.
- In Acadia, use designated campsites and avoid creating new ones. If camping in backcountry areas, choose durable surfaces like rock, gravel, or dry grass.

3. Dispose of Waste Properly:
- Carry out all trash, including food scraps and biodegradable waste. Use the park's waste disposal facilities or take your trash home.
- Follow the principle of "pack it in, pack it out." Proper waste disposal helps keep the park clean and safe for both wildlife and visitors.

4. Leave What You Find:
- Leave natural and cultural features undisturbed for others to enjoy. This includes not picking flowers, disturbing rock formations, or taking artifacts.
- Respect historical and cultural sites by not defacing or removing any objects.

5. Minimize Campfire Impact:
- Use a camp stove for cooking instead of building a campfire. If you must have a fire, use established fire rings and keep fires small.
- Gather firewood only if permitted and use only dead and downed wood. Extinguish all fires completely before leaving.

6. Respect Wildlife:
- Observe animals from a distance and avoid feeding them. Feeding wildlife can disrupt their natural behaviors and harm their health.

- Store food securely to prevent attracting animals to your campsite. In Acadia, use bear-proof containers if provided.

7. Be Considerate of Other Visitors:
- Respect the peace and solitude of others by keeping noise levels low. Yield to other hikers on trails and be courteous in crowded areas.
- Follow park regulations and guidelines to ensure a positive experience for everyone.

Eco-Friendly Accommodation and Dining

Choosing eco-friendly accommodation and dining options can significantly reduce your environmental impact while supporting sustainable practices.

Eco-Friendly Accommodation:

- Green Hotels: Look for accommodations that have eco-certifications or green practices in place, such as energy-efficient lighting, water-saving fixtures, and recycling programs. Many hotels in the Bar Harbor area, for example, participate in sustainable initiatives.
- Camping: Camping is an eco-friendly option, especially if you follow Leave No Trace principles. Acadia has several campgrounds that offer a low-impact way to stay in the park.
- Sustainable Lodging: Some lodges and bed-and-breakfasts use sustainable practices, such as sourcing local, organic food for their meals and using non-toxic cleaning products.

Eco-Friendly Dining:

- Local and Organic: Choose restaurants that serve locally sourced and organic food. This reduces the carbon footprint associated with

transporting food over long distances and supports local farmers.
- Sustainable Seafood: When dining in coastal areas like Acadia, opt for sustainable seafood choices. Look for certifications like the Marine Stewardship Council (MSC) label, which indicates that the seafood was sourced responsibly.
- Minimize Waste: When dining out, avoid single-use plastics by bringing your own reusable utensils, straws, and containers for leftovers. Many restaurants in eco-conscious communities are happy to accommodate these practices.

Supporting Local Communities

Supporting local communities not only enhances your travel experience but also contributes to the well-being and sustainability of the region.

Shop Local:
- Artisans and Crafts: Purchase souvenirs and gifts from local artisans and craft markets. This supports local economies and helps preserve traditional crafts.
- Farmers' Markets: Visit farmers' markets to buy fresh produce, baked goods, and other locally made products. This supports local farmers and reduces the environmental impact of food transportation.

Engage with the Community:
- Cultural Experiences: Participate in cultural tours and events that are led by locals. This provides a deeper understanding of the area's history and traditions while supporting local guides and businesses.
- Volunteer Opportunities: Some parks and communities offer volunteer programs that allow visitors to give back while enjoying their stay. This can include trail

maintenance, beach cleanups, and educational programs.

Support Local Businesses:
- Dining: Eat at locally-owned restaurants and cafes instead of chain establishments. This keeps money within the community and often provides a more authentic dining experience.
- Accommodation: Stay at locally-owned hotels, bed-and-breakfasts, or vacation rentals. These businesses are often more invested in sustainable practices and the well-being of their community.

Reducing Your Carbon Footprint

Traveling sustainably means being mindful of your carbon footprint and taking steps to reduce it.

Transportation:
- Public Transit and Shuttles: Use public transportation or park shuttles whenever possible. Acadia National Park offers a free shuttle service, the Island Explorer, which reduces the need for private vehicles and lowers emissions.
- Carpooling: If you must drive, consider carpooling with other travelers to reduce the number of vehicles on the road.
- Biking and Walking: Explore the park on foot or by bike. Acadia has an extensive network of carriage roads that are perfect for cycling and walking.

Energy Conservation:
- Turn Off Lights and Electronics: Conserve energy by turning off lights, heating, cooling, and electronics when not in use. Many accommodations have eco-friendly reminders and practices in place.

- Solar Chargers: Use solar-powered chargers for your electronic devices. This reduces the need for electricity and is particularly useful for camping trips.

Water Conservation:
- Short Showers: Take shorter showers to conserve water. Be mindful of water usage, especially in areas that experience drought conditions.
- Reusables: Use a reusable water bottle instead of buying bottled water. Many parks have water refill stations to encourage this practice.

By adopting these sustainable travel tips, you can help protect Acadia National Park and other natural destinations for future generations. Your efforts to minimize your environmental impact, support local communities, and reduce your carbon footprint make a significant difference in preserving the beauty and integrity of these treasured places.

Made in the USA
Monee, IL
15 August 2024